Charolette

God Bless you!

[signature]

PRAISE FOR

Complete FAITH

I have watched this book develop from day one. I have seen, first hand, God reveal Michelle's personal connection between His wisdom, her life, and her circumstance. The results live in the pages of this phenomenal devotional and have deeply impacted my relationship with God.

SHANNON STEWART

I'm so excited for you Michelle! This is evolved evangelism in my mind; adapting your message to fit this current generation and really spreading a meaningful, current word.

BRIANA J. ALLEN

You're giving birth to this book.

ANGELA COLTER

If you are looking to know more about God and his character, this is it! "Complete Faith" is a very necessary devotional, sparking spiritual and emotional growth. This journey spoke to me in every way I needed, while encouraging me in the pursuit of God. The author provided personable daily readings, with a spot-on application of the given scriptures. The prayers at the end of each day are short, sweet, and effective. I wholeheartedly recommend this devotional to any woman. If you're a non-believer, a baby in Christ, or straddling the fence, this is it! If you serve on every board in the church, this is it! No matter where you are, you owe it to yourself to take this 31 day journey. It will change your life.

CHYNA ROBINSON

Complete
FAITH

31 Days of Practical Teachings for Complete Faith in God

MICHELLE STEWART

COMPLETE FAITH - 31 Days of Practical Teachings for Complete Faith in God

Published by Michelle Stewart

Definitions are taken from www.dictionary.com or created by the author.

All scripture quotations are from the authorized versions of the bible referenced for each scripture.

ISBN-13: 978-0692368664

ISBN-10: 0692368663

Dedication

This book is dedicated to my children. You, whom I seek to inspire with my life, have inspired me the most through yours. I thank God for you. I am ever grateful for the privilege of allowing God to love you tangibly through my touch, daily by my actions and forever in your hearts and fondest memories.

I love you!

~Mommy (Nonny)

CONTENTS

INTRODUCTION

I am not a seasoned writer. I am not a scholar. I do not have the perfect past and I am not perfect now. I still struggle with things I face in life. I do not have all of the answers. However, as I write this devotional I am reminded of this one thing, I have had everything I will ever need since the moment I accepted Jesus Christ as my personal Lord and Savior. I am a wife and a mother of four amazing children. I am an evangelist, which is just a fancy way of saying that I LIVE for an opportunity to tell anyone about Jesus. We will only ever be as equipped for our journey in life as we are willing to devote time to learn the word of God. The power of His presence coupled with the power of his word, revealed to a yielded heart, is a phenomenal force to be reckoned with. I pray that as you read this devotional, you will become confident in the power of His indwelling presence in your life.

This book is a compilation of practical teachings paired with personal experiences. I am thrilled to share them with you. With complete faith it is time that we walk into the fullness of our purpose. Forsaking not the past which now propels us into a brighter future. Leaning not unto our own understanding, but pressing into and possessing the promises of God concerning us all. Let's Go! Join me for 31 days of devotion, deliverance, and complete faith!

FAITH

DAY 1

Hebrews 11:1 (NIV)

[1]Now faith is confidence in what we hope for and assurance about what we do not see.

Hebrews 11:1 (AMP)

[1]Now faith is the assurance (the confirmation, [a]the title deed) of the things [we] hope for, being the proof of things [we] do not see *and* the conviction of their reality [faith perceiving as real fact what is not revealed to the senses].

Faith

noun

1. Confidence or trust in a person or thing: *faith in another's ability.*
2. Belief that is not based on proof: *He had faith that the hypothesis would be substantiated by fact.*

Have you ever found yourself facing a problem that was beyond your ability to solve? Have you ever felt like you were sinking? It may have seemed like you were being drug down or consumed by a situation in your life. Maybe you feel like your current situation is causing you to drift further and further away from a place you once felt secure, as if being pulled away from shore. It may have taken you by surprise. Maybe you walked into a situation thinking that you could handle it on your own, or maybe someone left you to fend for yourself. Whatever the situation may be or have been, in that moment you realized that you would need help. At the very least you needed something to hold onto. If you can identify with one of these scenarios, at some point you may have been told to "just have faith". You may have even heard the phrase "keep the faith".

That's nice, right? But let's be honest… these phrases are useless if you don't know what faith is or how to use it.

Hebrews 11:1 (NIV) teaches us that faith is "confidence" in what we cannot see. It sounds easy enough but when you have been let down before, it's just not that simple. OR IS IT? When you lack that thing called confidence, HOW are you ever expected to grasp the concept of having faith?

Faith is like a floatation device filled with air. The plastic alone couldn't save you but once you fill it with air… you know, the stuff you can't see… IT CAN SAVE YOUR LIFE. IT CAN CHANGE YOUR SITUATION. IT MAY NOT BE VISIBLE, BUT IT IS CAPABLE.

Note: You can't float out of that bad situation with faith if you are still connected to an anchor. What do you need to let go of today?

Q&A

What is God saying to you?
_____

- ❖ What key words or verse stands out to you?
- ❖ What significance does it have in your life right now?
- ❖ How is God prompting you to apply this to your life?
_____

PRAYER~ Today, I pray that my faith will be activated through confidence. I pray that I will receive faith and put it to work in my life like the invisible air in a flotation device. I pray that faith will elevate me and allow me to see past the things that worry me ~In Jesus' name, amen.

FEAR

DAY 2

2 Timothy 1:7 (AMP)

⁷ For God did not give us a spirit of timidity (of cowardice, of craven and cringing and fawning fear), but [He has given us a spirit] of power and of love and of calm *and* well-balanced mind *and* discipline *and* self-control.

Fear

noun

1. a distressing emotion aroused by impending danger, evil, pain, etc., whether the threat is real or imagined; the feeling or condition of being afraid. Synonyms: foreboding, apprehension, consternation, dismay, dread, terror, fright, panic, horror, trepidation, qualm. Antonyms: courage, security, calm, intrepidity.

"Fight fear with FIERCE faith."

I recently posted a question on social media. I asked, *"What is keeping you from your dream?"* All of the responses were surprisingly similar. The root cause of each answer listed was fear.

Fear, simply put, is a strategy the enemy uses to distract, detour and ultimately destroy you. It is a battle that you can win only by taking your own thoughts captive.

Years ago, I struggled heavily with depression. I walked around every day with that lump in my throat and piercing emptiness in the pit of my stomach. I was beat down by the burden of condemnation and fear. The enemy was winning the battle that raged in my mind. I was desperate for God's comfort and restoration of peace but didn't know how to receive it. Finally, I tried something I had never attempted before. I decided to fast from negative thoughts. I decided to surrender my fears to God every single time they threatened to overwhelm me. As soon as a negative thought would come, I would force it out with prayer, songs of praise, worship and scripture. It is a process that I have since encouraged many women to adopt.

Do you struggle in this area? If so, I want to encourage you to fight your fears with fierce faith. My prayer is that you, too, will experience freedom from the bondage of fear. It's time to believe the truth that God promises for your future. Pick up your bible or open your bible app today and you will find victory and life changing revelation as you diligently study His word. Saturate your mind with scripture and drown out every deceptive thought fueled by fear.

5 DAY CHALLENGE

If you want to be released from overwhelming feelings of fear, this is a great way to begin. For the next five days, write in your Complete Faith Journal about something positive in your life. Write down what you are grateful for. You can also include an encouraging scripture.

Q&A

What is God saying to you?

- ❖ What key wordss or verse stands out to you?
- ❖ What significance does it have in your life right now?
- ❖ How is God prompting you to apply this to your life?

PRAYER~ Today, I pray that my fears will no longer keep me captive. Lord I surrender them all to you. I pray for revelation that will increase my faith as I claim victory over fear ~In Jesus' name, amen.

A BROKEN HEART

DAY 3

Psalm 34:18 (NLT)

[18] The LORD is close to the brokenhearted; he rescues those whose spirits are crushed.

Broken

adjective

1. Reduced to fragments; fragmented.
2. Ruptured; torn; fractured.
3. Not functioning properly; out of working order.

Once upon a time,

I totally believed that falling in love would be my own personal fairytale. I believed my first love would be my true and lifelong happily ever after experience. I believed that my belief in happy endings was enough. That in itself, it was powerful enough to conquer anything. I was wrong…

The thing about my favorite childhood fairytales is that they were all full of fantasy and magic, but void of the presence or even recognition of God. Would they really have you think that a life filled with so much favor was possible without Him? Wow! I was deceived! Been there?? I was waiting on a "prince" to rescue me when The Prince of Peace (Jesus) was waiting for ME to realize that He already had. If I had only looked to the word of God, I would never have been led into some of the darkest times of my life.

Have you ever had a broken heart? The moment you realize that you have given your heart to someone who never understood how to care for it, or simply didn't value it, is devastating. Love is powerful, yet it seemingly renders you powerless when given and never received. The absence of love in a relationship can reduce confidence to fragments and fracture hope. It can also cause you to manage future relationships improperly.

Has your broken heart, broken you? God wants to fix what's been broken. God wants to break you out of the bondage of brokenness today. Somebody needs change... but they don't want to be broken... am I making sense?

"Somebody needs change... but they don't want to be broken... am I making sense?"

God is going to use your broken heart to build an awesome testimony. It may be uncomfortable but the results will be incredible if left in His hands. The change you need will be made from the broken places in your life. There is truly such a thing as living happily ever after. It's called JOY. It's unconditional and it is a gift from God.

Q&A

What is God saying to you?

- ❖ What key words or verse stands out to you?
- ❖ What significance does it have in your life right now?
- ❖ How is God prompting you to apply this to your life?

PRAYER~ Lord, today I pray that You will break every chain of bondage connected to my broken heart. I pray that I will receive Your love and that it will set me free by penetrating every poisonous and deceptive plan the enemy has against my life. I give my heart to You ~In Jesus' name, amen.

FOCUS

DAY 4

Philippians 3:13 (NLT)

[13]No, dear brothers and sisters, I have not achieved it,[a] but I focus on this one thing: Forgetting the past and looking forward to what lies ahead,

Focus

noun

1.   A central point, as of attraction, attention, or activity:

Looking through a few old photo albums recently, I can remember looking at several pictures and squinting. It was as if I thought that by changing the way I looked at the blurred images, the images themselves would change. I was attempting to see them more clearly by changing my focus. However, changing my method of looking at a distorted image would never change that the image itself was in fact distorted.

In photography, the focus of the lens produces the image that will eventually be developed. If the focus is blurred, the image will be blurred. You will only be able to view things from the perspective in which that lens was able to capture. This is because the camera can only reproduce a clear image of what was in focus. My question is this: What blurred or distorted beliefs have you captured in your life and allowed to reproduce as your reality? What are you reproducing? (Ok, that was two questions, lol.) The point is, you will become what you behold.

"You will become what you behold"

If you are in an uncertain season or on a blurred path, I challenge you to stop trying to force it like me with those old photos. Ask God to correct the distorted image(s) in your mind by revealing the truth in His word.

Q&A

What is God saying to you?

- ❖ What key words or verse stands out to you?
- ❖ What significance does it have in your life right now?
- ❖ How is God prompting you to apply this to your life?

PRAYER~ Today, I pray that my focus in life will no longer be distorted by my past. I pray that I will see things as they truly are, and that You give me the proper perspective. Lord I want to see things like You do. Out of the richness of Your vision developed for my life, I will reproduce great things ~In Jesus' name, amen.

LOVE

DAY 5

1 John 4:7-10 (MSG)

God Is Love

[7-10] My beloved friends, let us continue to love each other since love comes from God. Everyone who loves is born of God and experiences a relationship with God. The person who refuses to love doesn't know the first thing about God, because God *is* love—so you can't know him if you don't love. This is how God showed his love for us: God sent his only Son into the world so we might live through him. This is the kind of love we are talking about—not that we once upon a time loved God, but that he loved us and sent his Son as a sacrifice to clear away our sins and the damage they've done to our relationship with God.

Love

noun

1. God

God loves you!

Until you truly know God, you have not truly experienced love.

It's funny because I thought I had, but what I experienced was full of imperfections. The thing I called "love" in the past was absolutely conditional even though God's word teaches that Love is not. What I experienced was weakened by circumstance and cheapened by lust.

So much of what I believed about love was shaped by the pop culture of my generation. I had no idea how off base I was, but often wondered why what seemed to work for everyone else wasn't working for me.

Hanging on to provocative and popular lyrics, my flesh was being moved by the seduction of sweet melodies. I was dancing right into a snare. Don't let the "love" songs of your favorite artists determine your expectations of love. You certainly do not have to be "Crazy", "Dangerously", or "Drunk" to experience #EPIC love.

"**You certainly DO NOT have to be**
(("Crazy")), "Dangerously",
or "Drunk" to experience #**EPIC**
love."

In fact, I believe these things were meant to deceive us so that when we finally received true love we wouldn't recognize it. Here's what love really looks like:

1 Corinthians 13:4-7 (NLT)

[4] Love is patient and kind. Love is not jealous or boastful or proud [5] or rude. It does not demand its own way. It is not irritable, and it keeps no record of being wronged. [6] It does not rejoice about injustice but rejoices whenever the truth wins out. [7] Love never gives up, never loses faith, is always hopeful, and endures through every circumstance.

Q&A

What is God saying to you?

- ❖ What key words or verse stands out to you?
- ❖ What significance does it have in your life right now?
- ❖ How is God prompting you to apply this to your life?

PRAYER~ Today, I pray that the love of God would fill my

heart and dispel every false belief I have ever received about love as truth
~In Jesus' name, amen.

DOUBT

DAY 6

Psalm 94:18-19 (NLT)

[18] I cried out, "I am slipping!" but your unfailing love, O LORD, supported me. [19] When doubts filled my mind, your comfort gave me renewed hope and cheer.

Psalm 94:18-19 (AMP)

[18] When I said, My foot is slipping, Your mercy *and* loving-kindness, O Lord, held me up. [19] In the multitude of my [anxious] thoughts within me, Your comforts cheer *and* delight my soul!

Doubt

verb (used with object)

1. To be uncertain about; consider questionable or unlikely; hesitate to believe.
2. To distrust.
3. (Archaic) to fear; be apprehensive about.

Doubt is a DREAM Killer

My doubt, my unbelief, kept me from giving 100% in several areas of my life -- including writing this book. Over the years, my inability to believe in myself has proven to be one of my greatest faults. I had allowed it to defeat me before, but this time I decided to believe God for a victory.

Doubt is a constant battle for many of us. Fighting through the fear of failure is often easier said than done. This is when you look to God. He can magnify your determination by renewing a right spirit in you. In the scripture the psalmist speaks of "slipping", BUT being supported by

24

God's "unfailing love". Let the love of God lead you. He has no desire to see you fail. Pray that your passions be paralleled with His, and that His dream, vision and purpose for you will become your own.

Jeremiah 29:11 (NLT) says, "For I know the plans I have for you," says the LORD. "They are plans for good and not for disaster, to give you a future and a hope."

Don't allow doubt to delay you another day. Doubt is a distraction that will lead you to a dead end. This is the day that God desires for you to choose victory. Keep pressing forward with hope toward a fantastic future!

Q&A

What is God saying to you?

- ❖ What key words or verse stands out to you?
- ❖ What significance does it have in your life right now?
- ❖ How is God prompting you to apply this to your life?

PRAYER~ Today, I pray that my hope in You Lord, and my trust in Your unfailing love will light my path. I pray that doubt will no longer possess the power to detour or delay my destiny ~In Jesus' name, amen.

PROCRASTINATION

DAY 7

Proverbs 12:24 (NLT)

24 Work hard and become a leader; be lazy and become a slave.

Procrastinate

verb (used without object)

1. To defer action; delay: to procrastinate until an opportunity is lost.

verb (used with object)

2. To put off till another day or time; defer; delay.

Live for TODAY like there is no

TOMORROW

Have you ever put something off for a day or two that somehow became ten? O_o I have. I'd personally mastered the art of procrastination at one point in my life. Do you want to know how? It's simple. I called it by another name, which was conveniently… "me time". Because of that name, I was able to justify it in my own mind. Telling myself that I deserved it, I deferred to it as often as I could. In hind sight I can totally see how the enemy played me. I was, in all essence, telling myself that I didn't deserve anything. Wow! I made myself so busy doing what I wanted to do that I was too busy for what I needed to do. Unfortunately there is no reward for being unproductive. Trust me, you can easily waste the majority of your life with mixed up priorities. People procrastinate in all areas of life. We put off education, committing to healthy habits, ending bad relationships and even spending time with God. I pray that your passion to be in God's presence will prevail over the power of procrastination.

"I pray that your passion to be in God's presence will prevail over the power of procrastination."

One of the biggest struggles in my Christian journey has been study, prayer and meditation on God's word. I started one year study plans and took two years to complete them. I worked all day, did nothing all night and fell asleep in prayer. I scrolled down social media news feeds for hours, then spent a few minutes here and there skimming through scriptures. I've been distracted, barely giving any attention to the audible voice of my bible app. I HAVE PROCRASTINATED... big time... and rendered myself powerless and ill-prepared when faced with unforeseen trials in life. If only my passion for the pages of scripture had been greater, I would have never put off the protection of God's word. You don't have to be a slave to procrastination. Master it by surrendering it to God.

5 DAY CHALLENGE

How can "Me time" become "He time?" Starting today, try giving that often wasted "Me time" to The Lord and spend some "He time." Here's how. Select five bible verses, and memorize one each day for the next five days. **You should definitely make this a priority even beyond our "He time" challenge. It will bless you! **

Can't think of any Bible verses to kick off this challenge? I've got you covered. ☺ Check out the list below.

- ❖ *Psalms 16:8 (NLT)*
- ❖ *Colossians 2:7 (NLT)*
- ❖ *Psalms 119:11 (NLT)*
- ❖ *James 1:2-3 (NLT)*
- ❖ *Hebrews 11:6 (NLT)*

What is God saying to you?

- ❖ What key words or verse stands out to you?
- ❖ What significance does it have in your life right now?
- ❖ How is God prompting you to apply this to your life?

PRAYER~ Today, I pray that my passion for scripture will be increased. Lord please deliver me from procrastination in every area of my life. I want to live for You today like there is no tomorrow ~In Jesus' name, amen.

WORSHIP

DAY 8

John 4:24 (NLT)

[24] For God is Spirit, so those who worship him must worship in spirit and in truth."

John 4:24 (MSG)

[23-24] "It's who you are and the way you live that count before God. Your worship must engage your spirit in the pursuit of truth. That's the kind of people the Father is out looking for: those who are simply and honestly *themselves* before him in their worship. God is sheer being itself—Spirit. Those who worship him must do it out of their very being, their spirits, their true selves, in adoration."

Worship

noun

1. Reverent honor and homage paid to God or a sacred personage, or to any object regarded as sacred.

Worship is not just the awesome mini concert preceding the sermon at Sunday morning service. It's not limited to the hands raised, tears flowing, emotional exhortation many of us render to God. Worship is a way of life. You can literally worship while you wait in line at the bank. You can worship at work or in class. You can worship while washing dishes. It really doesn't matter where you are. All that matters is that your heart is fully surrendered to God.

"Your worship must engage your spirit in the pursuit of truth."

The Message Bible says it beautifully, "Your worship must engage your spirit in the pursuit of truth." Notice that the scripture doesn't say that worship must engage you emotionally. So many of us are seeking God for something, often in worship, but receive nothing. Could this be why? Have we mistaken being moved emotionally for having an authentic spiritual encounter with the true and living God? If so, how do we enter worship in spirit? I believe it is through relationship. Real intimacy is experienced through relationship. How well do you know God? It's not good enough to just read His profile as if on social media or an online dating site. We MUST get to know Him in order to truly worship Him. Read your bible to learn His secrets. Don't just read to complete the one year reading plan you receive alerts for on your smart phone. Read the bible as if it were a love note written just for you. True love will bring you into the presence of God for true worship.

What is God saying to you?

- ❖ What key words or verse stands out to you?
- ❖ What significance does it have in your life right now?
- ❖ How is God prompting you to apply this to your life?

PRAYER~ Father, I want to experience worship like the scripture reveals. I want to worship in such a way that it engages both my spirit and Yours. Lead me deeper into relationship with You as I lean deeper into your holy word ~In Jesus' name, amen.

PURPOSE

DAY 9

Ecclesiastes 3:1 (KJV)

[1] To everything there is a season, and a time to every purpose under the heaven:

Proverbs 15:22 (AMP)

[22] Where there is no counsel, purposes are frustrated, but with many counselors they are accomplished.

Purpose

noun

1. The reason for which something exists or is done, made, used, etc.
2. An intended or desired result; end; aim; goal.

"ANYTHING that dares to exalt itself above my God and His purpose in my life will be DISMISSED."

Each day as I write this book, it becomes more evident to me that God desires to unveil His purpose in your life. It is time.

It is not your season sister… it is YOUR TIME. Seasons come in cycles, but an appointed time begins and then it ends. Consider this: there is a summer in every year, but June 2014 (a time)… #doneSon. Let God bless what He has already begun in you. You were born with power and purpose. Surround yourself with wise counsel, because it's time for you to walk in it. Declare that anything that dares to exalt itself above my God and His purpose in my life, will be dismissed.

Have you ever heard the saying, "You came into this world alone and you will leave it alone?" THIS IS A LIE. We came into being by the hand of God. We will transition from life to life eternal by the hand of God. So why shouldn't we walk each day of our lives CONNECTED to the hand of God? Ask the Lord to place the right people in your life. He is faithful and loving. If you thought you were waiting on Him, news flash -- He's been waiting on you. It is time for you to dismiss your distractions. Trust me... they were strategically positioned to lead to your destruction. We have all been gifted with time here. What are you doing with yours?

"It is time for you to dismiss your distractions. Trust me... they were strategically positioned to lead to your destruction."

Q&A

What is God saying to you?

- ❖ What key words or verse stands out to you?
- ❖ What significance does it have in your life right now?
- ❖ How is God prompting you to apply this to your life?

PRAYER~ Today, I pray that my time would be filled with Your purpose Lord. I want to live for You ~In Jesus' name, amen.

PURITY

DAY 10

Psalm 119:9 (NLT)

⁹ How can a young person stay pure? By obeying your word.

Purity

noun

1. The condition or quality of being pure; freedom from anything that debases, contaminates, pollutes, etc.: the purity of drinking water.
2. Freedom from any admixture or modifying addition.
3. Ceremonial or ritual cleanness.
4. Freedom from guilt or evil; innocence.
5. Physical chastity; virginity.

Day ten, purity. I must admit that writing on this subject was a challenge. I first asked the Lord why. I wondered why He would have me write about something that I had never mastered. I have struggled with living a life of purity throughout my entire Christian journey. It wasn't until now that I understood the depth at which the absence of this virtue has effect.

Purity is an ongoing process. It's like having an air purifier in a room. It only works if:

1. You know how to use it (read instruction manual)
2. It's connected to a power source
3. It's turned on/ Activated

So, if you are struggling in this area of your life, I have a few questions. Have you read the instructions (Bible)? Are you connected to your power source (Christ)? Remember the purifier cannot function without power.

Lastly, have you put the instruction to action in your life? What turns you on will determine how successful you become in this area. Pun intended.

Purity is a process. The function of a purifier is to continuously remove contaminants from an environment. It has to stay on to be effective. So, don't just "turn up" for Jesus. Turn on.

What is God saying to you?

- ❖ What key words or verse stands out to you?
- ❖ What significance does it have in your life right now?
- ❖ How is God prompting you to apply this to your life?

PRAYER~ Today, I pray that You will purify my heart Lord. I want to be so connected to You that a man would have to know AND obey your instructions to turn me on. Thank You for the power to live a life of purity ~In Jesus' name, amen.

THE REAL SELFIE CHALLENGE

Today, we will begin a 10 DAY challenge. On social media, posting a "selfie" (a picture of someone taken by that same someone) is very popular. These pictures are most often posted online for public view. I was thinking about how this concept could help us spiritually. After all, who doesn't like a good #selfie? For 10 days we will have focal scriptures to study. This is a time that you should pause and take a snap shot of your life.

Consider this: Where are you right now spiritually? Are you all dolled up, posing in a filthy room (environment)? Are you using all types of filters to mask and make your image appear better? Examining the image that you present to the world daily, ask yourself if it meet God's standard for His daughters. Better yet, is it really you? Unlike the selfies we post on social media, these selfies are not about what we look like; they are about what we live like.

Use each scripture as a filter to find what God wants to fix in your life. Answer the questions and journal daily about what God is speaking to you, about you. If you are active on social media, post and caption an actual selfie each day with the hashtags #TheRealSelfie and #CompleteFAITH. Let your light so shine unto this world through the power of your own daily walk with Jesus.

You will find that the daily scriptures come from different translations. I selected and shared some of my favs with you, but I also encourage you to read various translations for optimal understanding.

I pray that this challenge blesses you! ~ Michelle

(((Ready??? SET... GO!)))

THE REAL SELFIE 1

Day 11

2 Timothy 3:16-17 (NLT)

[16] All Scripture is inspired by God and is useful to teach us what is true and to make us realize what is wrong in our lives. It corrects us when we are wrong and teaches us to do what is right. [17] God uses it to prepare and equip his people to do every good work.

What is God saying to you?

---

* ❖ What key words or verse stands out to you?
* ❖ What significance does it have in your life right now?
* ❖ How is God prompting you to apply this to your life?

PRAYER~ Lord, I'm listening. As I study and search Your word, please search my heart and renew my mind. Speak Your heart to me and as You reveal it I pray for complete and unwavering faith in You ~In Jesus' name, amen.

THE REAL SELFIE 2

DAY 12

Romans 5:1-5 (AMP)

[1] Therefore, since we are justified (acquitted, declared righteous, and given a right standing with God) through faith, let us [grasp the fact that we] have [the peace of reconciliation to hold and to enjoy] peace with God through our Lord Jesus Christ (the Messiah, the Anointed One).

[2] Through Him also we have [our] access (entrance, introduction) by faith into this grace (state of God's favor) in which we [firmly and safely] stand. And let us rejoice *and* exult in our hope of experiencing *and* enjoying the glory of God.

[3] Moreover [let us also be full of joy now!] let us exult *and* triumph in our troubles *and* rejoice in our sufferings, knowing that pressure *and* affliction *and* hardship produce patient *and* unswerving endurance.

[4] And endurance (fortitude) develops maturity of character (approved faith and tried integrity). And character [of this sort] produces [the habit of] joyful and confident hope of eternal salvation.

[5] Such hope never disappoints *or* deludes *or* shames us, for God's love has been poured out in our hearts through the Holy Spirit Who has been given to us.

Q&A

What is God saying to you?

- ❖ What key words or verse stands out to you?
- ❖ What significance does it have in your life right now?
- ❖ How is God prompting you to apply this to your life?

PRAYER~ Lord, I'm listening. As I study and search Your word, please search my heart and renew my mind. Speak Your heart to me and as You reveal it I pray for complete and unwavering faith in You ~In Jesus' name, amen.

THE REAL SELFIE 3

DAY 13

Psalm 13 (MSG)

A David Psalm

13 ¹⁻² Long enough, GOD—
    you've ignored me long enough.
I've looked at the back of your head
    long enough. Long enough
I've carried this ton of trouble,
    lived with a stomach full of pain.
Long enough my arrogant enemies
    have looked down their noses at me.

³⁻⁴ Take a good look at me, GOD, my God;
    I want to look life in the eye,
So no enemy can get the best of me
    or laugh when I fall on my face.

⁵⁻⁶ I've thrown myself headlong into your arms—
    I'm celebrating your rescue.
I'm singing at the top of my lungs,
    I'm so full of answered prayers.

Q&A

What is God saying to you?

- ❖ What key words or verse stands out to you?
- ❖ What significance does it have in your life right now?
- ❖ How is God prompting you to apply this to your life?

PRAYER~ Lord, I'm listening. As I study and search Your word, please search my heart and renew my mind. Speak Your heart to me and as You reveal it I pray for complete and unwavering faith in You ~In Jesus' name, amen.

THE REAL SELFIE 4

DAY 14

2 Corinthians 12:8-10 (AMP)

[8] Three times I called upon the Lord *and* besought [Him] about this *and* begged that it might depart from me;

[9] But He said to me, My grace (My favor and loving-kindness and mercy) is enough for you [sufficient against any danger and enables you to bear the trouble manfully]; for *My* strength *and* power are made perfect (fulfilled and completed) *and show themselves most effective* in [your] weakness. Therefore, I will all the more gladly glory in my weaknesses *and* infirmities, that the strength *and* power of Christ (the Messiah) may rest (yes, may pitch a tent over and dwell) upon me!

[10] So for the sake of Christ, I am well pleased *and* take pleasure in infirmities, insults, hardships, persecutions, perplexities *and* distresses; for when I am weak [in human strength], then am I [truly] strong (able, powerful in divine strength).

Q&A

What is God saying to you?

❖ What key words or verse stands out to you?

❖ What significance does it have in your life right now?

❖ How is God prompting you to apply this to your life?

PRAYER~ Lord, I'm listening. As I study and search Your word, please search my heart and renew my mind. Speak Your heart to me and as You reveal it I pray for complete and unwavering faith in You ~In Jesus' name, amen.

THE REAL SELFIE 5

Psalm 27 (NLT)

A psalm of David.

[1] The LORD is my light and my salvation—
so why should I be afraid?
The LORD is my fortress, protecting me from danger,
so why should I tremble?
[2] When evil people come to devour me,
when my enemies and foes attack me,
they will stumble and fall.
[3] Though a mighty army surrounds me,
my heart will not be afraid.
Even if I am attacked,
I will remain confident.

[4] The one thing I ask of the LORD—
the thing I seek most—
is to live in the house of the LORD all the days of my life,
delighting in the LORD's perfections
and meditating in his Temple.
[5] For he will conceal me there when troubles come;
he will hide me in his sanctuary.
He will place me out of reach on a high rock.
[6] Then I will hold my head high
above my enemies who surround me.
At his sanctuary I will offer sacrifices with shouts of joy,
singing and praising the LORD with music.

[7] Hear me as I pray, O LORD.
Be merciful and answer me!

[8] My heart has heard you say, "Come and talk with me."
And my heart responds, "LORD, I am coming."
[9] Do not turn your back on me.
Do not reject your servant in anger.
You have always been my helper.
Don't leave me now; don't abandon me,
O God of my salvation!
[10] Even if my father and mother abandon me,
the LORD will hold me close.

[11] Teach me how to live, O LORD.
Lead me along the right path,
for my enemies are waiting for me.
[12] Do not let me fall into their hands.
For they accuse me of things I've never done;
with every breath they threaten me with violence.
[13] Yet I am confident I will see the LORD's goodness
while I am here in the land of the living.

[14] Wait patiently for the LORD.
Be brave and courageous.
Yes, wait patiently for the LORD.

Q&A

What is God saying to you?

- ❖ What key words or verse stands out to you?
- ❖ What significance does it have in your life right now?
- ❖ How is God prompting you to apply this to your life?

PRAYER~ Lord, I'm listening. As I study and search Your word, please search my heart and renew my mind. Speak Your heart to me and as You reveal it I pray for complete and unwavering faith in You ~In Jesus' name, amen.

THE REAL SELFIE 6

DAY 16

Psalm 32 (NLT)

A psalm of David.

¹ Oh, what joy for those
    whose disobedience is forgiven,
    whose sin is put out of sight!
² Yes, what joy for those
    whose record the LORD has cleared of guilt,
    whose lives are lived in complete honesty!
³ When I refused to confess my sin,
    my body wasted away,
    and I groaned all day long.
⁴ Day and night your hand of discipline was heavy on me.
    My strength evaporated like water in the summer heat. Interlude

⁵ Finally, I confessed all my sins to you
    and stopped trying to hide my guilt.
I said to myself, "I will confess my rebellion to the LORD."
    And you forgave me! All my guilt is gone. Interlude

⁶ Therefore, let all the godly pray to you while there is still time,
    that they may not drown in the floodwaters of judgment.
⁷ For you are my hiding place;
    you protect me from trouble.
    You surround me with songs of victory. Interlude

⁸ The LORD says, "I will guide you along the best pathway for your life.
    I will advise you and watch over you.
⁹ Do not be like a senseless horse or mule
    that needs a bit and bridle to keep it under control."

¹⁰ Many sorrows come to the wicked,
   but unfailing love surrounds those who trust the LORD.
¹¹ So rejoice in the LORD and be glad, all you who obey him!
   Shout for joy, all you whose hearts are pure!

Q&A

What is God saying to you?

- ❖ What key words or verse stands out to you?
- ❖ What significance does it have in your life right now?
- ❖ How is God prompting you to apply this to your life?

PRAYER~ Lord, I'm listening. As I study and search Your

word, please search my heart and renew my mind. Speak Your heart to me and as You reveal it I pray for complete and unwavering faith in You ~In Jesus' name, amen.

DAY 17

John 3:16-17 (AMP)

[16] For God so greatly loved *and* dearly prized the world that He [even] gave up His only begotten (unique) Son, so that whoever believes in (trusts in, clings to, relies on) Him shall not perish (come to destruction, be lost) but have eternal (everlasting) life.

[17] For God did not send the Son into the world in order to judge (to reject, to condemn, to pass sentence on) the world, but that the world might find salvation *and* be made safe *and* sound through Him.

What is God saying to you?

- ❖ What key words or verse stands out to you?
- ❖ What significance does it have in your life right now?
- ❖ How is God prompting you to apply this to your life?

PRAYER~ Lord, I'm listening. As I study and search Your word, please search my heart and renew my mind. Speak Your heart to me and as You reveal it I pray for complete and unwavering faith in You ~In Jesus' name, amen.

THE REAL SELFIE 8

DAY 18

Luke 11:1-13 (MSG)

Ask for What You Need

11 One day he was praying in a certain place. When he finished, one of his disciples said, "Master, teach us to pray just as John taught his disciples."

2-4 So he said, "When you pray, say,

Father,
Reveal who you are.
Set the world right.
Keep us alive with three square meals.
Keep us forgiven with you and forgiving others.
Keep us safe from ourselves and the Devil."

5-6 Then he said, "Imagine what would happen if you went to a friend in the middle of the night and said, 'Friend, lend me three loaves of bread. An old friend traveling through just showed up, and I don't have a thing on hand.'

7 "The friend answers from his bed, 'Don't bother me. The door's locked; my children are all down for the night; I can't get up to give you anything.'

8 "But let me tell you, even if he won't get up because he's a friend, if you stand your ground, knocking and waking all the neighbors, he'll finally get up and get you whatever you need.

9 "Here's what I'm saying:

Ask and you'll get;
Seek and you'll find;
Knock and the door will open.

10-13 "Don't bargain with God. Be direct. Ask for what you need. This is not a cat-and-mouse, hide-and-seek game we're in. If your little boy asks for a serving of fish, do you scare him with a live snake on his plate? If your little girl asks for an egg, do you trick her with a spider? As bad as you are, you wouldn't think of such a thing—you're at least decent to your own children. And don't you think the Father who conceived you in love will give the Holy Spirit when you ask him?"

Q&A

What is God saying to you?

- ❖ What key words or verse stands out to you?
- ❖ What significance does it have in your life right now?
- ❖ How is God prompting you to apply this to your life?

PRAYER~ Lord, I'm listening. As I study and search Your word, please search my heart and renew my mind. Speak Your heart to me and as You reveal it I pray for complete and unwavering faith in You ~In Jesus' name, amen.

THE REAL SELFIE 9

DAY 19

Philippians 3:7-14 (AMP)

[7] But whatever former things I had that might have been gains to me, I have come to consider as [one combined] loss for Christ's sake.

[8] Yes, furthermore, I count everything as loss compared to the possession of the priceless privilege (the overwhelming preciousness, the surpassing worth, and supreme advantage) of knowing Christ Jesus my Lord *and* of progressively becoming more deeply *and* intimately acquainted with Him [of perceiving and recognizing and understanding Him more fully and clearly]. For His sake I have lost everything and consider it all to be mere rubbish (refuse, dregs), in order that I may win (gain) Christ (the Anointed One),

[9] And that I may [actually] be found *and* known as in Him, not having any [self-achieved] righteousness that can be called my own, based on my obedience to the Law's demands (ritualistic uprightness and supposed right standing with God thus acquired), but possessing that [genuine righteousness] which comes through faith in Christ (the Anointed One), the [truly] right standing with God, which comes from God by [saving] faith.

[10] [For my determined purpose is] that I may know Him [that I may progressively become more deeply and intimately acquainted with Him, perceiving and recognizing and understanding the wonders of His Person more strongly and more clearly], and that I may in that same way come to know the power outflowing from His resurrection [which it exerts over believers], and that I may so share His sufferings as to be continually transformed [in spirit into His likeness even] to His death, [in the hope]

52

¹¹ That if possible I may attain to the [spiritual and moral] resurrection [that lifts me] out from among the dead [even while in the body].

¹² Not that I have now attained [this ideal], or have already been made perfect, but I press on to lay hold of (grasp) *and* make my own, that for which Christ Jesus (the Messiah) has laid hold of me *and* made me His own.

¹³ I do not consider, brethren, that I have captured *and* made it my own [yet]; but one thing I do [it is my one aspiration]: forgetting what lies behind and straining forward to what lies ahead,

¹⁴ I press on toward the goal to win the [supreme and heavenly] prize to which God in Christ Jesus is calling us upward.

#

What is God saying to you?

- ❖ What key words or verse stands out to you?
- ❖ What significance does it have in your life right now?
- ❖ How is God prompting you to apply this to your life?

PRAYER~ Lord, I'm listening. As I study and search Your word, please search my heart and renew my mind. Speak Your heart to me and as You reveal it I pray for complete and unwavering faith in You ~In Jesus' name, amen.

THE REAL SELFIE **10**

DAY 20

Jeremiah 29:11-12 (NLT)

¹¹ For I know the plans I have for you," says the LORD. "They are plans for good and not for disaster, to give you a future and a hope. ¹² In those days when you pray, I will listen.

Romans 5:3-6 (NLT)

³ We can rejoice, too, when we run into problems and trials, for we know that they help us develop endurance. ⁴ And endurance develops strength of character, and character strengthens our confident hope of salvation. ⁵ And this hope will not lead to disappointment. For we know how dearly God loves us, because he has given us the Holy Spirit to fill our hearts with his love.

⁶ When we were utterly helpless, Christ came at just the right time and died for us sinners.

What is God saying to you?

- ❖ What key words or verse stands out to you?
- ❖ What significance does it have in your life right now?
- ❖ How is God prompting you to apply it to your life?

PRAYER~ Lord, I'm listening. As I study and search Your word, please search my heart and renew my mind. Speak Your heart to me and as You reveal it I pray for complete and unwavering faith in You ~In Jesus' name, amen.

TRUST

DAY 21

Philippians 4:11-13 (NLT)

[11] Not that I was ever in need, for I have learned how to be content with whatever I have. [12] I know how to live on almost nothing or with everything. I have learned the secret of living in every situation, whether it is with a full stomach or empty, with plenty or little. [13] For I can do everything through Christ, who gives me strength.

Trust

noun

1. Reliance on the integrity, strength, ability, surety, etc., of a person or thing; confidence.
2. Confident expectation of something; hope.
3. Confidence in the certainty of future payment for property or goods received; credit:

It's easy to trust God when things are going great. It's easy when there's a full fridge, a steady pay check, the sun is shining, the marriage is marvelous, good health, good grades, no drama, etc. However, we live in a world full of uncertainties. We live in a world full of suffering and it becomes a bit more difficult to trust God as He (seemingly) stands by with all power, yet He uses none. In a world where cancer is often a victorious villain and we mourn the mass murder of children, many prayers seem to go unanswered. It is in this world that we must remain optimistic, not being overcome by the paralysis of pessimism. It is in times like these that we must live the revelation Paul shares with us in Philippians. We must trust God, NOT just in spite of the circumstance. We must trust God WITH the circumstance. Paul says that he learned the secret of living in every situation. This is key: He said "living in" not living through. More often than not, we are more concerned with what's to come than what is. This is that moment you decide to trust God... no matter what.

"That moment you **decide** to ((*trust God*)) no matter what."

What is God saying to you?

* ❖ What key words or verse stands out to you?
* ❖ What significance does it have in your life right now?
* ❖ How is God prompting you to apply it to your life?

PRAYER~ Father I want to trust You no matter what I face. Today, I surrender my cares to You. I pray that my confidence in You will never fail ~In Jesus' name, amen.

PRAYER

DAY 22

Philippians 4:6-7 (NLT)

[6] Don't worry about anything; instead, pray about everything. Tell God what you need, and thank him for all he has done. [7] Then you will experience God's peace, which exceeds anything we can understand. His peace will guard your hearts and minds as you live in Christ Jesus.

Prayer

noun

1. A devout petition to God or an object of worship.

Finding Peace Through Prayer~

Recently I was asked to speak at a prayer breakfast. The theme was Finding Peace Through Prayer. As I pondered the scripture and the theme, a few things began to stand out.

First, we often seek to find peace in prayer rather than "through" prayer. Have you ever been told to "just pray about it" when you were going through a tough time or facing a tough decision? The advice would cause you to think that there is actually peace in the prayer itself. However, prayer is NOT the solution; it is the connection with the one who has the solution.

Secondly, I was reminded of another scripture about prayer. It's one of my favorite stories in the Bible because it really hit home for me in a sensitive time in my life. In Mark 9, Jesus is approached by a man with a demon possessed child. The man had already taken the child to the disciples but they had not been successful in their attempts to solve the man's problem. His son was still possessed. (Ever taken your problems to a spiritual leader and still found no peace? No solution? BEEN THERE!) Before delivering the boy from his demons Jesus asked the man if he believed.

"The father instantly cried out, I do believe but help me overcome my unbelief!" Mark 9:24

Do you really believe that God can do what you're asking? Are you not sure that He will? BELIEVE, and ask God to help you overcome what you cannot, your unbelief.

Finally, the story ends with Jesus simply commanding the demons to come out of the child. Immediately after, his disciples asked why they were unsuccessful in their efforts to help the man and his child.

"Jesus replied, this kind can be cast out only by prayer."

Funny thing is, Jesus never once paused to pray in this scripture. I was floored when I realized this. I thought, Wow! What does this mean?

We struggle finding peace through our prayers because we wait until the problem, the dilemma, or the disaster has come into our life to pray about it. Jesus has shown us that we can't wait until we are facing a problem to ask God for the solution. We need it now!

"That **moment** when your **prayers** become

PRO-active instead of RE-active...

((GAME CHANGER))."

Think about that for a moment. How different would things be if you were prepared in advance? How confident would you be if you had already spoken to God about your problem? That moment when your prayers become PRO- ative instead of RE-active... GAME CHANGER.

You will have peace through a proactive prayer life. Your solutions are all waiting in His presence. Go, and go often. Don't wait until the problem comes. Prepare now so that you can have peace as you overcome. This peace truly surpasses all understanding.

 Q&A

What is God saying to you?

- ❖ What key words or verse stands out to you?
- ❖ What significance does it have in your life right now?
- ❖ How is God prompting you to apply it to your life?

PRAYER~ Lord, I surrender my cares to you in advance. I have decided to trust You no matter what. Today, I am asking for what only You know that I will need tomorrow ~In Jesus' name, amen.

ANXIETY

DAY 23

Philippians 4:4-9 (AMP)

[4] Rejoice in the Lord always [delight, gladden yourselves in Him]; again I say, Rejoice!

[5] Let all men know *and* perceive *and* recognize your unselfishness (your considerateness, your forbearing spirit). The Lord is near [He is coming soon].

[6] Do not fret *or* have any anxiety about anything, but in every circumstance *and* in everything, by prayer and petition (definite requests), with thanksgiving, continue to make your wants known to God.

[7] And God's peace [shall be yours, that tranquil state of a soul assured of its salvation through Christ, and so fearing nothing from God and being content with its earthly lot of whatever sort that is, that peace] which transcends all understanding shall garrison *and* mount guard over your hearts and minds in Christ Jesus.

[8] For the rest, brethren, whatever is true, whatever is worthy of reverence *and* is honorable *and* seemly, whatever is just, whatever is pure, whatever is lovely *and* lovable, whatever is kind *and* winsome *and* gracious, if there is any virtue *and* excellence, if there is anything worthy of praise, think on *and* weigh *and* take account of these things [fix your minds on them].

[9] Practice what you have learned and received and heard and seen in me, *and* model your way of living on it, and the God of peace (of untroubled, undisturbed well-being) will be with you.

Anxiety

noun

1. Distress or uneasiness of mind caused by fear of danger or misfortune: He felt anxiety about the possible loss of his job.
2. Earnest but tense desire; eagerness: He had a keen anxiety to succeed in his work.

I have dealt with anxiety for as long as I can remember. I'm not sure how it started. I would randomly feel completely overwhelmed and uneasy. My husband would often speak awesome words of encouragement to me and they were full of love. I still dealt with this feeling that I could not seem to shake. The problem was I didn't know why I felt that way. I only knew how "it", whatever "it" was, made me feel.

"We actually believe that muting the symptoms of our circumstances is deliverance."

In our world, we've learned to treat the symptoms. There are so many over the counter meds to treat cold "symptoms", allergy "symptoms" etc. We actually believe that muting the symptoms of our circumstances is deliverance. We have been deceived. Philippians 4:4-9 offers peace in place of the problem raging in your thought life. You don't have to take anything. You only need to give. Give God your petition. Anxiety is the earnest but tense desire for help. If you've ever experienced this feeling you know that it is consuming. If you've ever had to treat cold or allergy symptoms you know that it is best to prepare in advance. Get vaccinated or take the necessary precautions in advance. Prayer works that way. You don't have to wait until it hurts. Go to God now for what you need tomorrow.

Q&A

What is God saying to you?

- ❖ What key words or verse stands out to you?
- ❖ What significance does it have in your life right now?
- ❖ How is God prompting you to apply this to your life?

PRAYER~ Today I pray that my symptoms, my concerns, my fears, my earnest and tense desires, my uneasiness will become subject to the scripture Philippians 4: 4-9. It is my prayer. I desire to receive the peace of God in place of these problems ~In Jesus' name, amen.

WHAT IS DEVOTION?

DAY 24

Joshua 1:8-9 (NLT)

[8] Study this Book of Instruction continually. Meditate on it day and night so you will be sure to obey everything written in it. Only then will you prosper and succeed in all you do. [9] This is my command—be strong and courageous! Do not be afraid or discouraged. For the LORD your God is with you wherever you go."

Devotion

noun

1. Profound dedication; consecration.
2. Earnest attachment to a cause, person, etc.
3. An assignment or appropriation to any purpose, cause, etc.

Can I be honest? I hope so… because I have personally, always struggled with spending time in "devotion" to God. Crazy huh? Especially since I am writing this one for you (hehe). This is one of the reasons that I now know that God placed writing a devotional in my heart. It has been through this process that I have come to TRULY understand the often untapped treasure we have in our ability to spend time in the presence of God. We can learn of Him FROM HIM. The creator of ALL things, the only true and living God, the all-powerful and all-knowing God, our redeemer, actually wants to spend HIS TIME with us! YET, we often need to be pushed or provoked by our problems into His presence. Why?

I believe that this is just a part of the enemy's plan. If he can keep us from spending time with God he can keep us from ever experiencing the gift of relationship with God. It is because of the enemy's attitude toward God that he is now and forever out of the bond of a love relationship with God. Satan wanted the glory that he was created to give to God. So it is fitting that he would stop at nothing to keep us from experiencing God in this way. Devotion IS relationship. It is real and it is only as powerful in our lives as WE allow.

"Revelation FROM God comes from relationship WITH God."

How deep have you gone into relationship with God? What if I told you that your success was in His presence? Your peace is in His presence. Your unconditional joy is in his presence. Your identity and purpose will ONLY be found and brought to its full potential in His presence. Eternal life was the rebate for surrendering your life to its manufacturer. Devotion is the only place that honors the unwavering warranty, the protection plan of His love. Devotion is relationship and relationship is the reason for it all. God loves you.

Q&A

What is God saying to you?

- ❖ What key words or verse stands out to you?
- ❖ What significance does it have in your life right now?
- ❖ How is God prompting you to apply this to your life?

PRAYER~ Lord, as I enter your presence today, let it be a time that I experience relationship with you in ways that I never have before. I want to know You more personally and intimately. My Lord, my God, my Father, and my Friend, I value our time together and I pray that I will never neglect it but make priority of it, as long as I live ~In Jesus' name, amen.

TELL YOUR STORY

DAY 25

John 4:28-30 (AMP)

[28] Then the woman left her water jar and went away to the town. And she began telling the people,

[29] Come, see a Man Who has told me everything that I ever did! Can this be [is not this] the Christ? [Must not this be the Messiah, the Anointed One?]

[30] So the people left the town and set out to go to Him.

Tell

verb (used with object), told, telling.

1. To give an account or narrative of; narrate; relate (a story, tale, etc.): *to tell the story of Lincoln's childhood.*
2. To make known by speech or writing (a fact, news, information, etc.); communicate.
3. To announce or proclaim.
4. To express in words (thoughts, feelings, etc.).
5. To reveal or divulge (something secret or private).
6. To say plainly or positively

Who knew that there were so many ways to define the word "tell"? Not me... O_o

This is such a vital topic, because so many people are locking the less attractive parts of their lives -- their testimonies, their triumphs over trouble, their story -- away in a prison called "privacy". More often than not, they justify the silence and refuse to tell (testify to) anyone. We live in a day where redemptive unedited truths are amiss.

"We **live** in a day where **redemptive** unedited **truths** are amiss."

In today's scripture reading, the woman (well known as the Samaritan woman) has a one on one personal experience with Jesus. During their conversation, Jesus exposed her troubled past and her present problem (living with a man that was not her husband... yeah... go read John 4... it's juicy lol)

I love how Jesus does this. He exposes her faults but does not condemn her. Jesus came to SAVE!

It was by telling her story (vs. 28-29) that a whole town eventually knew where to find the savior. She told everybody about Jesus.

I want to encourage you to do the same. Tell your story. Tell somebody where you met Jesus. YES! Where, not just how or when. The Samaritan woman met Jesus at a well, yes, but we learned where she was in life when she met Jesus.

Where were you when you met Jesus? Were you delivered or rescued from an ugly place in life. Were you a spiritual wreck? Maybe you were spiritually void. You may be experiencing Jesus for the first time right now, as you read this devotional. Whatever the case may be, Jesus met with you (is meeting with you) because He wanted to. Go and tell the town, your family, the town, your coworkers, the town, your friends, the town, a stranger. Tell "the town" that it doesn't matter who they are, where they've been, or what they did. Jesus wants to meet them too.

This week's challenge is to encourage someone. Tell them about a time when knowing God had the most impact on your life, and if they don't know Jesus, tell them where they can find Hm. (See Bonus Day 32: Salvation)

Q&A

What is God saying to you?

- ❖ What key words or verse stands out to you?
- ❖ What significance does it have in your life right now?
- ❖ How is God prompting you to apply this to your life?

PRAYER~ Father, thank You for my story. Just like the Samaritan woman did, I want to tell someone where they can find You. I pray that You will begin to place people in my life so that I can lead them to You ~In Jesus' name, amen.

CULTIVATING YOUR CRAFT

DAY 26

Jeremiah 29:11 (NLT)

¹¹ For I know the plans I have for you," says the LORD. "They are plans for good and not for disaster, to give you a future and a hope.

Colossians 3:23

Amplified Bible (AMP)

²³ Whatever may be your task, work at it heartily (from the soul), as [something done] for the Lord and not for men,

Cultivate

verb (used with object), cultivated, cultivating.

1. To develop or improve by education or training; train; refine: to cultivate a singing voice.
2. To promote the growth or development of (an art, science, etc.); foster.
3. To devote oneself to (an art, science, etc.).

I had my fourth child this year. Our first boy. He's just two months old now, but full of the favor, anointing and promises of God. I'm so in love with my children. As I'm writing now, he is playing with the toys that I connected to his seat, the kind that dangle overhead just within arm's reach. This made me think of our walk with God. I believe that God places things and people in our lives that we need for development. I believe that just as I placed the toys close enough for my baby to reach, God places everything we need within our reach. The problem is, to many of us never reach out and grab those things. We play around but never fully capture what God so desires for us to possess.

As an infant you need someone to give things to you. When you grow up, more often than not, you have to go get it for yourself. As you are reading this, you ought to be able to identify which stage you're in. Are you an infant or an adult? Has God given you a gift, a sense of purpose, or an identity to cultivate? What are you doing to develop it now? Are you cultivating your craft or are you still playing with it?

God loves you and has a plan for you. He doesn't want you to work for Him. He wants you to work with Him. Whatever it is that you are gifted to do, do it as unto the Lord.

What is God saying to you?

- ❖ What key words or verse stands out to you?
- ❖ What significance does it have in your life right now?
- ❖ How is God prompting you to apply this to your life?

PRAYER~ Lord, it's me again. Thank you for creating me with purpose. I pray that I will never miss an opportunity to grow closer to fulfil it. I pray for the wisdom necessary to manage it well and to recognize everything, every person, every decision, and every resource that you provide along the way ~In Jesus' name, amen.

OBEDIENCE

DAY 27

John 14:21 (AMP)

21 The person who has My commands and keeps them is the one who [really] loves Me; and whoever [really] loves Me will be loved by My Father, and I [too] will love him and will show (reveal, manifest) Myself to him. [I will let Myself be clearly seen by him and make Myself real to him.]

Obey

verb (used with object)

1. To comply with or follow the commands, restrictions, wishes, or instructions of: *to obey one's parents.*
2. To comply with or follow (a command, restriction, wish, instruction, etc.).
3. (of things) To respond conformably in action to: *The car obeyed the slightest touch of the steering wheel.*
4. To submit or conform in action to (some guiding principle, impulse, one's conscience, etc.).

So… Did you know that obedience is a definitive act of love…?!?!? Wow! Right?

As I consider all of the times in my life that I was NOT obedient to the word of God, I realize that I was telling God that I didn't love him more than I loved myself. O_O I was obedient to my own will. I was submissive to my own desires. I was loving myself to death when God so desperately wanted to love me to life.

"I was **loving** myself **to death** when God so desperately **wanted to** **love** me to **life**."

What are your actions saying to God? What or who are you submissive to other than Him? Too many of us walk around with this false and warped sense of security. We convince ourselves that the statement, "God knows my heart", means that He will accept a heart that is not yet yielded to Him. Yes, God examines the heart, but He also knows our intentions. The bible says in Psalm 139, He knows our "…thought afar off." So our intent will never be a substitute for being obedient. It's time to choose Him and serve Him through the loving response of obedience.

#

What is God saying to you?

* ❖ What key words or verse stands out to you?
* ❖ What significance does it have in your life right now?
* ❖ How is God prompting you to apply this to your life?

PRAYER~ Father, please forgive me. I pray that even my intent is to be obedient to You. Lord I pray that my actions and my thoughts communicate love to You ~In Jesus' name, amen.

SATISFACTION

DAY 28

John 6:35 (AMP)

³⁵ Jesus replied, I am the Bread of Life. He who comes to Me will never be hungry, and he who believes in *and* cleaves to *and* trusts in *and* relies on Me will never thirst any more (at any time).

Matthew 5:6 (AMP)

⁶ Blessed *and* fortunate *and* happy *and* spiritually prosperous (in that state in which the born-again child of God enjoys His favor and salvation) are those who hunger and thirst for righteousness (uprightness and right standing with God), for they shall be completely satisfied!

Satisfy

verb (used with object)

1. To fulfill the desires, expectations, needs, or demands of (a person, the mind, etc.); give full contentment to: *The hearty meal satisfied him.*
2. To put an end to (a desire, want, need, etc.) by sufficient or ample provision: *The hearty meal satisfied his hunger.*
3. To give assurance to; convince: *to satisfy oneself by investigation.*
4. To answer sufficiently, as an objection.
5. To solve or dispel, as a doubt.

Have you ever eaten a whole meal but somehow felt a need for more? Have you craved a specific sweet treat but had to settle for what was in the fridge or pantry at home? In these instances you are not hungry or thirsty but there is still a void. You are seeking satisfaction. Likewise, spiritually we often consume and digest enough to be full but still find ourselves less than satisfied. We long for more, but more of what? I believe that often in life we have misunderstood our cravings. We fill

73

ourselves with whatever is laying around in the pantry, developing an appetite for temporary sinful satisfaction. "Many of us don't eat or drink for nourishment. We consume things for the sake of satisfaction."

"Many of us don't eat or drink for nourishment. We consume things for the sake of satisfaction."

In today's scripture, we find that Jesus has the recipe, the secret ingredients that will forever solve this problem. Jesus offers Himself. You may be saying to yourself, I have already received Jesus. But do you still crave things that are not good for you? Keep consuming Christ, the bread of Heaven until you hunger and thirst no more. Commit spiritual gluttony by binging on the bible. Snack on the scriptures. Don't settle, be satisfied every day.

Q&A

What is God saying to you?

- ❖ What key words or verse stands out to you?
- ❖ What significance does it have in your life right now?
- ❖ How is God prompting you to apply this to your life?

PRAYER~ Father, from this day forward, I will seek you alone for satisfaction. Thank you for sending Your son Jesus for both my deliverance and my delight ~In Jesus' name, amen.

ACCOUNTABILITY

DAY 29

James 5:16 (AMP)

16 Confess to one another therefore your faults (your slips, your false steps, your offenses, your sins) and pray [also] for one another, that you may be healed *and* restored [to a spiritual tone of mind and heart]. The earnest (heartfelt, continued) prayer of a righteous man makes tremendous power available [dynamic in its working].

Hebrews 12:14-16 (AMP)

14 Strive to live in peace with everybody and pursue that consecration *and* holiness without which no one will [ever] see the Lord.

15 Exercise foresight *and* be on the watch to look [after one another], to see that no one falls back from *and* fails to secure God's grace (His unmerited favor and spiritual blessing), in order that no root of resentment (rancor, bitterness, or hatred) shoots forth and causes trouble *and* bitter torment, and the many become contaminated *and* defiled by it—

16 That no one may become guilty of sexual vice, or become a profane (godless and sacrilegious) person as Esau did, who sold his own birthright for a single meal.

Accountable

adjective

1. Subject to the obligation to report, explain, or justify something; responsible; answerable.

I have found that having someone to hold me accountable for my actions, reactions, responses, and thoughts in regard to certain issues in my life to be paramount. Why? It's simple. Left to my own emotions, I would be full of regret, blinded by what I could see rather than being guided by what I could not. I've done so many bad things and made so many bad decisions while being blinded by circumstance. I needed another pair of eyes on the issues life presented to me but for the sake of privacy, saving face......... I looked only to myself. Have you ever been there? You know, that moment if there had been just one trustworthy voice of reason in your corner, you would have made a different decision? That moment when you decided to take a risk. That moment when you probably knew better but since no one was around to object or (let's be real) witness, you did IT... whatever IT was. This is called accountability.

We all need people in our lives that will pull us aside when we are wrong and push us through with encouragement to do what's right. The problem is, often times, we end up resenting the ones who take a stand against the way that SEEMS right to us. We push them away or flat out ignore what they have to say. In the end we feel much more than resentment. We feel regret. Can you recall a time in your life when having someone like this present would have been beneficial? Can you identify someone in your life right now who can hold you accountable to the standard God is calling you to live? If so, thank them and thank God for them. If not, ask God to send them. They will bless your life!

Q&A

What is God saying to you?

- ❖ What key words or verse stands out to you?
- ❖ What significance does it have in your life right now?
- ❖ How is God prompting you to apply this to your life?

PRAYER~ Father I come to You now, asking that You will positon the right people in my life. Lord, I want to be the me that you created me to be. Help me to recognize the people you want me to trust when I am weakest. Use our relationships for your glory ~In Jesus' name, amen.

YOU MATTER

DAY 30

John 3:16 (KJV)

[16] For God so loved the world, that he gave his only begotten Son, that whosoever believeth in him should not perish, but have everlasting life.

Jeremiah 29:11 (NLT)

[11] For I know the plans I have for you," says the LORD. "They are plans for good and not for disaster, to give you a future and a hope.

You

noun

1. Whomever God created you to be. This is what defines you.

When the Lord placed this topic in my heart for today's entry, I realized that the problem I have struggled with for most of my life wasn't just my own. My parents divorced when I was eleven, and I felt an overwhelming sense of rejection. I spent years seeking to be affirmed and accepted by men through a series of bad... no, REALLY BAD relationships. I tried to fit in with whatever crowd would receive me. I began to feel like being me, wasn't ever going to be good enough. I had to be better. I needed to be what people wanted me to be. I had to be somebody else. I needed to be someone who mattered. Why was being me never enough? I was always getting left behind, picked over or not chosen at all.

God shared His heart for each of us who have ever felt cast aside. He wants you to know that, "YOU MATTER" to Him. Yes, you! If you have ever felt insignificant. If you've felt inadequate, unqualified, unwanted, unloved, unworthy, un_____ Un_____ UN_____, you fill in the blanks. God wants to assure you today that YOU MATTER to

Him and that is ALL THAT MATTERS. God gave His only son FOR YOU, and He has plans FOR YOU. You couldn't be more significant if you tried my friend.

"God wants to assure you today that YOU MATTER to Him and that is ALL THAT MATTERS."

Q&A

What is God saying to you?

- ❖ What key words or verse stands out to you?
- ❖ What significance does it have in your life right now?
- ❖ How is God prompting you to apply this to your life?

PRAYER~ Father, thank You for thinking of me. I needed to know that not only do I believe in You, but YOU believe in ME. Help me to live my life worthy of one who matters to You ~In Jesus' name, amen.

MOTIVATION

DAY 31

Colossians 3:23-24 (AMP)

[23] Whatever may be your task, work at it heartily (from the soul), as [something done] for the Lord and not for men,

[24] Knowing [with all certainty] that it is from the Lord [and not from men] that you will receive the inheritance which is your [real] reward. [The One Whom] you are actually serving [is] the Lord Christ (the Messiah).

Motivation

noun

1. Something that causes a person to act in a certain way, do a certain thing, etc.; incentive.
2. The goal or object of a person's actions:

I recently received a.... well let's just say… lengthy text message from someone that made me ponder their motives. It made me wonder how often in life motive is really contemplated. I was careful not to jump to conclusions, but what I saw seemed divisive. I didn't understand why. Had this person misunderstood my motives at some point? Had I inadvertently given a bad impression? If so, I thought, how can I avoid this in the future?

Outside of the common court room vernacular, motive is still a very powerful thing to consider in life. People pass major judgment on a person with perceived bad motives. Managing your motives is an excellent way to avoid conflict. If we always managed them as if unto the Lord, as the scripture suggests, we will experience more victories each day.

So, what is motivating you? Are you angry? Hurt? Jealous? Prideful? Afraid? Find out what God wants from you and let the Master manage your motives.

"Find out what God wants from you and let the Master manage your motives."

Q&A

What is God saying to you?

- ❖ What key words or verse stands out to you?
- ❖ What significance does it have in your life right now?
- ❖ How is God prompting you to apply this to your life?

PRAYER~ Today, I pray that Your motivation would become my own. Lord I surrender my will to You in this area ~In Jesus' name, amen.

BONUS DAY

SALVATION

Romans 10:9-11 (AMP)

[9] Because if you acknowledge *and* confess with your lips that Jesus is Lord and in your heart believe (adhere to, trust in, and rely on the truth) that God raised Him from the dead, you will be saved.

[10] For with the heart a person believes (adheres to, trusts in, and relies on Christ) and so is justified (declared righteous, acceptable to God), and with the mouth he confesses (declares openly and speaks out freely his faith) *and* confirms [his] salvation.

[11] The Scripture says, No man who believes in Him [who adheres to, relies on, and trusts in Him] will [ever] be put to shame *or* be disappointed.

Salvation

noun

1. The act of saving or protecting from harm, risk, loss, destruction, etc.
2. The state of being saved or protected from harm, risk, etc.
3. A source, cause, or means of being saved or protected from harm, risk, etc.
4. *Theology.* Deliverance from the power and penalty of sin; redemption.

I thought a long time about what I should say here. I just couldn't find words that seemed profound, really deep or thought provoking enough. These were the kinds of words I briefly felt were necessary to share this message with you. Then I remembered how I came to the most amazingly significant decision I've ever made. No one had to write a salvation sales pitch for me. Besides, my words could NEVER make Jesus more appealing than He already is. I acknowledged, confessed and received salvation through Jesus Christ fourteen years ago. Today, you can too. It's simple. Jesus is available to you and desires more than anything to save you and spend eternity loving the hurt off of you, the lies, the shame, the loneliness, the disappointment and the guilt. If you want Him, you can have Him.

The scriptures are true. Accepting Jesus Christ as your personal Savior is the condition connected to the promise that is revealed in Romans. Salvation is a promise that God has kept for us all. The question is, will you accept it?

If you are anything like me, you have either lived through or are currently in a season where you feel the depth of the need for something life changing. This is it.

Take a moment to read the prayer aloud if you would like to receive salvation or if you want to rededicate your life to Christ. Yes, it's that simple. ☺

"This is it!"

PRAYER~ Lord, I believe in my heart that Jesus died on the cross and rose from the grave to save me. I confess that I am not perfect. I have sinned, but now I know that You love and accept me anyway. Thank You for the gift of salvation! ~In Jesus' name, amen.

WHAT'S NEXT

Now that you've completed this devotional -- what's next? If you prayed and received Jesus as your savior today, I AM SO EXCITED FOR YOU!! This is only the beginning. God loves you and has GREAT things in store for your life. I encourage you to get connected with a local Bible based church. Join a small group ministry. Continue studying the scriptures. Journal each day, and continue growing in your faith. ~Michelle

Made in the USA
Charleston, SC
03 August 2015